I0203385

FREE VERSE EDITIONS
Edited by Jon Thompson

PILGRIMAGE SUITES

Derek Gromadzki

Parlor Press
Anderson, South Carolina
www.parlorpress.com

Parlor Press LLC, Anderson, South Carolina, 29621

© 2017 by Parlor Press
All rights reserved.
Printed in the United States of America
S A N: 2 5 4 - 8 8 7 9

Library of Congress Cataloging-in-Publication Data

Names: Gromadzki, Derek, author.
Title: Pilgrimage suites / Derek Gromadzki.
Description: Anderson, South Carolina : Parlor Press, [2017] |
Series: Free verse editions
Identifiers: LCCN 2017038925| ISBN 9781602358645
(pbk. : alk. paper) | ISBN   9781602358669 (epub) | ISBN
9781602358676 (ibook) | ISBN 9781602358683
    (mobi)
Classification: LCC PS3607.R636 A6 2017 | DDC 811/.6--
dc23
LC record available at https://lccn.loc.gov/2017038925

2 3 4 5

Cover design by Joshua Unikel.
Cover illustration by Frank Parker. Courtesy of Judith Parker.
    Used by permission.

Printed on acid-free paper.

Parlor Press, LLC is an independent publisher of scholarly and
trade titles in print and multimedia formats. This book is available
in paperback and ebook formats from Parlor Press on the World
Wide Web at http://www.parlorpress.com or through online and
brick-and-mortar bookstores. For submission information or to
find out about Parlor Press publications, write to Parlor Press,
3015 Brackenberry Drive, Anderson, South Carolina, 29621, or
email editor@parlorpress.com.

Contents

ACKNOWLEDGMENTS

Thanks to the editors of the following publications, in which many of the poems that follow first appeared, provisionally titled and often in rather different forms: *American Letters & Commentary*; *Black Warrior Review*; *The Brooklyner*; *The Buenos Aires Review*; *Colorado Review*; *Conjunctions*; *CutBank*; *Drunken Boat*; *Free Verse*; *Front Porch*; *The Journal*; *Midway*; *Monongahela Review*; *New Delta Review*; *Nimrod*; The PEN Poetry Series at PEN USA; and *Sakura Review*. Further thanks to John Cayley, Forrest Gander, Shane Mc-Crae, Gale Nelson, and Cole Swensen, for their insight during the writing of this book, and to Joshua Unikel for realizing its design.

A great debt of gratitude is owed to Judith and Diantha Parker, wife and daughter of the artist, Frank Parker. Frank created the images that accompany and punctuate, either as frontispieces or covers, Robert Lowell's books. And he created them largely in response to Lowell's poems. Through a strange reversal, after years spent reading those poems, I can imagine the images without them; I cannot imagine the poems without the images. May that and the reappearance of one of those images on the cover of this book – by Diantha's help and by Judith's permission – be another testament, however small, to the singular verve of Frank's hand. Thank you.

PILGRIMAGE SUITES

Him as was has gone from we
Us as is must go to he

—Inscribed on a Radnorshire gravestone

Overland

ICH EM NU ALDER ÞENE ICH WES, A WINTRE ENT A LARE,
ICH WELDE MARE ÞENE ICH DEDE, MI WIT AHTE BON MARE.

Bend a lay on a hamstrung broom

Upend your empty casks and bang

Abrasive on the drums of infidels

Mewl O imprudent voyagers mewl

And brag to rebec strings a fool's

Errand danced unshod for penance

Linger for the tune of wood that leads cicada song
in flight from fields   pipe soft   and charm these steps
           on ways not lost but loss   itself
                              where   the air turns air to silver
and opens fornever with nothing below first   patterns of asterisms unfolding
    — reel lie down   lie   down on the
                              wings of swifts   wheeling
              where remainders and the cast off symmetry of circles
              descend in   hymns

on a kind of mire   or slow mix of faith and idleness
   mortar shims and stonemen's brick   languishing under the influence of the sun
                         that parts spires from halls   until they fall from traditions
        to heath to houses of peat and clay
cracks filled with fishbone plaster
daubed with wine   and   the
                     haptic afterlapse of a grace held in scallop shells
                             drawn along the thews of melody
     dissembling and reassembling scant histories
       run through psalms whispered into rosewood beads
                   are rovers' odes for plowmen

accustomed to tides and the reaches of would-be
terrains scraped grim on tides' attritions
undoing   after us
              what we with twigs and slapdash ever did our
              weirs they swill apart they drift   down rindles
mixed among the sticklebacks and we   failed fishers too   we were
our soft wood rattling waves where eddies catch
         decay and ongoing corrosion
                   at lengths of damp advance a sterterous cringe
              through clabber we drag through clabber we   barely

as far as faded up from sleepless nods fortnights of present
    pass and we under wych elms   at the rim of limits recall
                              an incoherence not before or since
      seen came sat with longing   went
   for wilds of jackdaw feathers
                    hoar harrow lines and trees that command their costs
                              from beggared minds
                                    grudged to flight the first to stutter
                            unlettered and speak among mutes

we hoot transhumance and the march of souls
sojourning sick in blisters
foraged through food's elision never
did we settle here but were and we have been
down eroded runnels turned to crust
on the threadbare twitch of a hem
meanwhile bundles
of thicket brush rough and past our shins
wearing us worn across unadorned stores of rock
until our mouths touch dust
proceeding on bent knees we founder

drinking from cupped hands   we drink   weather   from water
  and impossible airs of surface move through us   in the sounds that children prate
                              — we the where   where the wind goes home
            guilty of spring and spring's beginnings
      unbound from the barley awn
                  pivot in range of thistle — may our bowers be willow be moss be glen
                        and the anomy these steps
                                          owe to rowans
                              shuffle grit and churn through seasons ceding

dusks to a hue of blind   through which we flinch
    sometimes   when a chill warps the weft of our clothes   we shake
            — roamed long through widow's weed
our feet   fallen to gossip in the foxglove
  speak with the sweetness of tongues   swallowing pollen
                    — quick stroke of sinews
      after corollas   the alar flits of toes and onward
    immerge in margins like

Matte black veneer a filter for transit

Padded a whip on a tailor's stitch

And knit the wale of a jackleg drawl

Say sheep thread unfurl say tinsel

Fray loose and crane raglan into the

Russet brogue wisps keen to wisps

Woe woe toll the threaves of indigo

Strum gravel seams undone and sew

Tithes for passage to sackcloth coats

Toss a pence for merchant saints

Cough your salt cant and a bellows

Sigh blow powder from your chests

On   carry   on   as   rain   respires   drifting
                    into celandine and sheds of sorts of
oxblood   leather   hemic
where hail and honey meet   the tint is this
                of rough boards   like   sticks laced inter and among each other
                    so many so many as the splinters on a broken branch
indifferent to the order of their grain
            are   disorder outstripped
                                its ruction   a prolonged exposure
                    that draws   the otherwise outside in

by where glades give on   glades and give open
                    onto a marsh it sinks our progress we start
  to move moving   slow as slumber
— we fight back a sinister of bites and stings
               for silence about the space of twice two days' balsam and salve
                              in beds of flax under a thatch roof
                              we footprint here soft weakened gaits
     with waterskins dead weight for water and
       nearby sits a stillness
                          quiet   witness to favor   so still
                              as straggling runs us ablur of sturdy

lower lowering still a simple swerve like mercy turns
                                        and grasps for gusts
            set wailing our regret
at ridges clouds have carved
                            ground to one single insistent drone of taking
                                stop on step alight off vigils of syllables
                incurable numb
            through short muttering voices
                        we offer our fathers

held up to a fire's glare
that greed of evening strips to embers
brittle idols split for kindling in   this cold only
eldritch onsets blink   and they with the grays of late
scattered ashes laid out trembling after
what orisons are had here last pit against a fixed immensity
— ears as eyes
eyes wider than sight
we hear how far the wayside carries

aware mere earth is the dearth through which mist advances
white flowers wet in the fens
we wade for leagues
of landscape where chill midges'
wingbeats freeze the runs of flesh around our ears —
shoulders shuddering we sleep
our tents too thin
betray us early to the light
and constellations end

the offing   its return between a shape
and shapes an edge so else the turf foot-shod drops paces on our heels
            — loose with slight   halts   faltering
                                takes itself apart with a twist of the   wrist
                                      around   widdershins
            wards   away the remains of rheum following
       to fold us spent   against   westwork granite
                             etched in the measure   of our origins
                       onto   shrill fulfillment and   what stirs beneath

mirrors   the thresh that holds a world   expels   these lungs   swelling
a double's rise — grips on anamnesis
                    covet meander its listless duration of want once wanted
   when   sense rocks back to an old safe place
   there comes an intrusion of the same uneven even as before
                                  these easeful halves lunged dumb
                    into pitch that   flickers inward in a bitter current
         as nightly currents pass   they
                    rub our meuse from our resemblance

Jawbone bismuth lathe a cackle on

Lodestone tines and sling your yarns

Now revel aloud for folly dragging

Behind the drayman and his dray

Dare the cart track from the clay

And splint your ankles with axel pins

CATHEDRA

MEST AL ÞET ME LIKEDE ER, NU HIT ME MISLIKEÐ
ÞA MUCHEL FULIEÐ HIS WIL, HINESOLF HE BISWIKEÐ.

Vellum indulgence and signet coils

Hem ribands around a counterfeit

Gift beholden by grievance to fever

Bitten tongues for forked contrition

Traffic with weepers of benediction

And grimly speak in subtle hells

Murmur sift incomplete and sudden —
    spring on   bowed feet
                            and lend no purchase to the flagstone floors
                these   our inhospitable welcome
    to the imprints of numberless   penitents crawling
sieved are we   like sand with trips and busted strides
                                    that impart digressions
                            tangled in riddles of empty

chant that unseals the eventide
and we suppose a posture from the curvetone tethered
                    to idle   heights   and swoon beneath hieratic
          scratches scratched on capitals   in the recesses
      lean among posts and
                    jambs hammered upright and we   we veer scavenging
                              chevrons for spheres' proportions where
          catenaries trail outlandish prodigies   and we commit to stray

so remote our imagination aiming at oblivions construes
        scales of the actual peculiar to exaltations of fling and whim
                            that elegance strangles
        from a lute's neck
strings up on transparent notes and plays like phosphor in the tempered glow
                        — minutes out of time when time was short
hover pluck and thrum tallow glister
        through opaque frames for the morrow mass
                    and croon O patiently patiently misapprehend

another chorder's cords unstrung to atone
for routed octaves clustered in the architraves
                    lanced under canopies without means to luster
                        gone from us as gone before a harmony
            that difference rifts and tumbles disenchanted
but in stooping we perceive
    how instinct beats in the skeleton's rattling pulse
                    and unrest of flesh a final prayer
                        threads us through us and through again

                              to enter by lintels   left
           hands of covenants not upheld —
                          here is meddle   more than dreams
and movement among unmoving things
      closes in falling   away a
                          closer letting go from the homeward road
             we are come to carved and savage stares displaying
                                      all   our   outcomes
                      on the backtrack crux of tracery
      crumbling in rude heaps
             at these doors and ways
          oblivious   this
                      a whimper of the omens
                              there are for if

summons   presence from upturned intervals and our
vows confound   unruly in a fume's pale clamor
enchanted-lanterned like nosuchplace
no such   when
a nave of haymakers heavy to buckle
deep slouch and crowded rummage
and we call to stars like living things
among the columns

while the pillars' high fill   burns   lambent   flames
                                    wasted   for   psalmody
     as   echoes   in the crooked coins we   carry
in   spare   scrips   flee   us   pursue   us
                                    sweeping   centers   crossing   out   from   form
        whole unrooms   of   labyrinths
                    contour   collide   and   dissolve   lidless
                        on   unquiet   eyes   so   near

Harbor above umber a dull accord

With undisciplined prose and ward

Your physic welter with stiff tisanes

Tremors in a pinch of ambergris

Tenor to storax and the hiss doubt

Blows like leaflets on your cheeks

Or to restart from sunder missing

Terms for thirst and purblind cling

To crude trinkets in the mulling dark

Rasp out parched over beads you

Clasp together with shepherd hooks

Tricks of chantry and a stifled token

Jagged duration and indecisions in a threshold gasp
    as the pepper of incense approaches
                oblique contortions in no positive hue to breach
                    trance and transience suborned
      by the merit of these many relics
when oil and oil's scents were story enough
                  a viscous quickening
among disused sentences and intonations from solitude
where things maintain the limits of actions
         and we of what composure if not of lumen
      brushed from columbine that ends on altars

in keener demarcations than forms of farewell
strange natures   that made us parts of ourselves
                                        retire disquiet to a twist
            on the screws of doxy
            and swill deep drafts of fog intermingling with afterimage
stranded on miscast regard   and inevitable error
against a feverish wish and a want like porcelain
                  here before hearing ceased or almost and humming
                              visions   set a rival up to

rites declined   from immanence and inclination
                                    spin rippled looks that comb
               over surfaces at angles tangent to our own
and hang on silent to the censer's inscription
      in open aisles   swung depended from undeterred
                                    ties at the invention of vapor
                     with word and gesture gesture and faint   predictions
                                    we bend to furnish bent decrees
      escape into chime and hesitate
            among finials stalled in final bloom
                     as the rushlights dwindle and commit to fetters

                        holes on behalf of cinerary resistance
            flicker a caprice of orbs and amber distilled in   lanterns
                  kindled   to charcoal sockets that deposit their lees onto our
listening and our cries singed by wicks   aspire to distended beacons
        sooner than fray
                    reverts to advent and attared wax
                                    ideas of circle top out   shallow
                            slipping   away from absolutes across
                sextons' tufts that collect the dead in points like lines

lines   like arcs and wending we widen in wonder
below circumspect cross sections of ashlar chutes
                    and lissome whists   around corkscrew shadows
                            to hazard a glance at patched atmosphere
                            as radiance stains through a glass   lightly
with all the fragile mimicry of life in pictures —
    how saints have bent slender here
                            under orisons and absence
                    over which appearance tips   and we the steadying

motley processions to promises   trippingly
pronounced   concerning   spaces
                    or the escape from spaces into learned verse
  for the learned and ruth for those who fumble through depiction
      spilled onto windowpanes too eagerly
                              grist for the diversions of crystal
                        abate   affect with a makeshift kilter

          and into grooves
      defile from lunettes trussed too briefly

to specter contingent too briefly
held for ideals only becoming by unlimited chance
we resign our exhalations to iron arms
that trail from chiseled figures
hiraeth figures on their haunches that affix a quivering leer
to oratory ungently divined by alchemical keys
enigmas in tinctures of mercury
asperge our antiphons released in-
distinct unto ellipses

Fain for emblems in dun perfume

Stains and fractures vacant under

Scenes arrayed in pendant slivers

Leaded be your laughter with metal

Bands pricked by a twinge of nettles

And all your cosseted song be lame

Waygate

WIS IS ÞE TO HIMSOLVE ÞENCH, ÞE HWILE ÞE HE MOT LIBBEN,
FOR SONE WULE HINE FORȜETEN ÞE FREMEDE ENT ÞE SIBBE.

Idle invite mischief and name a place

Tendrils of flatsedge call companion

To sweat leveraged in tumbril ruts

Dip foundering into the liquid tinge

Of a wheeze for a while and dredge

Up mercy from your hornpipe reeds

Waver out from rust and recite the incisions of arcades
          sourced   thinly   through   hushes
                                    borne deciphered from oleander
                              scrolls and lists of simples that texture
genuflection blown on rumors
      that blur stained patchwork fabric lapping at sepia pools
                              in reverberations strained to bring the sea
      strained we   sink
      away from foundations and rebuild footpaths
                    sintering a mineral persistence we quiver our confession is
                    tall grasses like taut wire against our calves

retold in disfigurations of endris cenoby
                        this that tempts is a breeze that suffers us
                                at the incarnadine fore of not in front
                    this too   is loss and quietly
furrows drone distant idylls
        testament to goatherd   tales
                                lolling scrawl blackthorn and write of skin
                        or should our retellers have told untrue

simply and in paler shades of somber
          as moments to millstones ride discarded
on the fossil shingles of oyster feasts
 and bridge the span we dance to cross could we
                  pick clean our careless afterthought
          to find a service for the dissent of crimson
      streaked howbeit over undergrowth
   shot lewd and tilting away from the dialect of logans
    gibbering of living lorn we   clamber

after augury's flights   we   lure   from   sour   flutes
                    the spar revisits white   in salt and onion skins
        and   leaguers
our peripheries like switchbacks   to   provoke
    migrations that void the stores of chaste   intent
                                enfold us into steepled greens and preach
                                        strange sooth   may shed a reign
                        and part a feather from its spell   it

flags on updrafts
          our wills whipsaw scoring and score us backwards
                    back from rags
                              worn out to tatters that storms fly after —
                    not to touch but   to be torn or touch
a while in fits — so few pleasures pass between us save for warmth
    in endless fields where we came
                                    where we continue and we have lain
                              cradled us we've lain in hills

at milestone marks driven we slip
and slip forward sideways to show the morning
run until unselved and
dry on droughts like cinders aside
where rivers tear from faith with their banks
off and over roads hardly road
signposts pitch visions and shrines
wait shrugging
in months of dusk
is how we are wan together

drawn to know no different direction
　　when long desires
　　　　　　　　　and vigors seep awash no way from back
　　　　　　　　　　　at outskirts' sight — to have   seen afar
　　　　　cast aspers on our trust
and seen from heaps of all and after slow
　　　　　　　　　　slowly depart this way
　　　　　　　　　　　we're in's a ceaseless forgetting
　　　creased with the press of always
　　　　a   diminishing instant distance fails

Traipse treble breaths on a double

Ground twice staked by sprain level

With buried lullabies and bandages

Waxed with ceresin candlesticks to

Vex the changeling aitches from

Hallows said for unhallowed bones

Uproot weight to weigh less to usher

Routes that aim returns and stagger

Uncontrolled ahead as if thrust back

Ever err aching for new moons that

Bear old moons in their arms and

Slink bedward by moonlight tapers

Easy reverence as age breaks ruin — or only just
        drudges vespers from a
                        season of trinities and division
                    not unlike a likeness to a fierce emergence
    from soundless encounters and the fugitive drift of bells
sways aimless into walking   waking
                        on ribs relaced with hunger
            and at our backs dark forms of belief and design

curl pewter we truckle they   chafe
                            and clink   dying the angelus   choirs
        defer a milder levin to   meridians
propped on   mattocks and   picks
                      we   change   our   throats from supplication
                                                lay our pleas astray
                          and fasten our legs
                            with leather and refugee blessings

                        wound from tartary lisle
          unwinding by short suddens
between itinerant limps and   convictions
                                        quit outstretched in the mud
                         and in our mudded paces where we huddle
          arrears in residence where we   reside
dialed on desolate   silhouettes
                  toward all our going and some feelings felt like vertigo

loop shoestring motions through the labor of leaves
        with a sense of smoke and raveling we grab
and plait our chilblain fingers through like
  copper rings for remembrance to keep from losing when
                they're gone as we lose watching
                    horizons release small reveries
        on an inkhorn map of chapels and byres

plotted on strokes of drystone fences low wicket
                gates around our knees where skirlings lour
and wait long hours to seize
the yawns of unfilled cisterns and unsettle the settled lichen
               on the wet latches that we tremble to catch
         to finish so little in leaving and having left
     stayed ordinary after weathered descents
        ascend our faces

                and a languor checks
                   our furtherance for

rival eithers   we arrive intruding
after the linseed and the dew's diversions
    spread in preface to a work to make
                        believe the blue whistles in pining
                    for facets of the familiar —
we have wicker crutches   and contritions
and we thumb our decades slow — unbroken stasis
                            of the broken
            chasing our own insteps on
                curves resurfaced from firmaments
                            to overlay   that

by twos twinning we unbecome
we under welkin we lumber
not ceased to be what   was
is wished until it were again once more
a rupture that peat bleeds phthisic in rivulets one
before into another after
harps altered water and returns a beryl din
flush this side of harm
where liar position takes and retakes its place

Tarry tell of wayfare and the way of

Ware that asks not earnest notes but

Shouts of fair misgivings that fiddle

A rhyme and pray a palmer's kiss

Kneel on hobnails and play at myths

With a bootstrap chorus of peddlers

About the Author

Derek Gromadzki is the recipient of an MFA in poetry from the Literary Arts Program at Brown University and an MFA in literary translation from the Translation Workshop at the University of Iowa, where he is currently a PhD candidate in comparative literature. His latest translations, collaborations with Sayuri Okamoto, can be found in *Alice, Iris, Red Horse: Selected Poems of Yoshimasu Gozo* (New Directions, 2016).

FREE VERSE EDITIONS

Edited by Jon Thompson

Signs Following by Ger Killeen
Split the Crow by Sarah Sousa
Spine by Carolyn Guinzio
Spool by Matthew Cooperman
Summoned by Guillevic, translated by Monique Chefdor & Stella Harvey
Sunshine Wound by L. S. Klatt
System and Population, by Christopher Sindt
These Beautiful Limits by Thomas Lisk
They Who Saw the Deep by Geraldine Monk
The Thinking Eye by Jennifer Atkinson
This History That Just Happened by Hannah Craig
An Unchanging Blue: Selected Poems 1962–1975 by Rolf Dieter Brinkmann,
    translated by Mark Terrill
Under the Quick by Molly Bendall
Verge by Morgan Lucas Schuldt
The Wash by Adam Clay
We'll See by Georges Godeau, translated by Kathleen McGookey
What Stillness Illuminated by Yermiyahu Ahron Taub
Winter Journey [Viaggio d'inverno] by Attilio Bertolucci, translated by
    Nicholas Benson
Wonder Rooms by Allison Funk

www.ingramcontent.com/pod-product-compliance
Lightning Source LLC
Chambersburg PA
CBHW022040090426
42741CB00007B/1138

* 9 7 8 1 6 0 2 3 5 8 6 4 5 *